A cwtch ir

Simone Mansell Broome

Cover by Cerys Susannah Rees

ISBN 978-1-8384580-3-4

Printed in the UK

Acknowledgements

An earlier version of ‘No rain in the desert’ was included in the anthology ‘A Star fell from Orion’ in November 2011. Thank you, belatedly, to Lampeter Writers’ Workshop for including me. ‘Elvis, an encounter’ was published in the Wildfire Words ezine in November 2022. Thank you to the Wildfire Words team for this.

Almost all the rest came mostly from a lost-and-found notebook.

Thanks are due as always to Roger, and to Cerys Susannah Rees who created the super cover illustrations.

The fire has been rekindled!

Foreword

This little volume of poems started as a notebook, a kind of journal, written on a holiday to Kyrenia. My daughter had just got married on our farm, in our wedding venue. To our chef. Which had been, for a small family business, challenging logistically. Their wedding, on October 6th, was the last of that season.

We'd hosted a variety of weddings that year, including the Elvis themed one – which had felt like an odd event to be happening in a West Wales field. It was our second year of weddings and it was beginning to look as though this new venture could succeed. We were also becoming aware what hard work was involved, how all-consuming in time and energy it would become.

When your child marries on your premises you wear multiple hats. It's a joyous experience but a stressful one too. In our case, once the newlyweds had left for a honeymoon in Sicily, it was time for us to have a little decompression. In Kyrenia.

Contents

Hiatus

Gull

Never a good idea to approach a wedding
with a hangover, before the event.
There's distant thunder, sky feathered with cloud.
Vesna, at the pool bar, sports two o'clock stubble,
more bristle than shadow, jet black,
but her hair, rubber-banded in bunches,
is the colour of grappa. Where it was still,
parasols ripple, edges of a yellow awning
flutter, flex, undulate, snap like sails.

Our order was cheese toasties, hoping grease would
mop up last night's excesses, but it comes laced
with unwanted ham donated by knife or board,
neither clean. We slide our plates under loungers,
untouched. Olive, mustard, ivory, sand,
oil paint splatters on concrete slabs –
these are the shades of shit excreted
by the one-footed gull inching closer. *No, we've got*
no food for you. He cocks his head to one side,

pecks at a powdery brown stain on paving,
drips from a choc ice, long since dried, hops to the pool,
drinks deep from chlorined blue, takes off, lopsided.
Days later you tell me how he came back,
the morning after, a balcony crash landing, startled you
as you watched the day stir, gain momentum,
me dead to it all in a crumple of bedding.
Trying it on, again, he was, that aerial chancer,
blown by gusts, storm clouds gathering.

Island wedding

We've not been spelled by wizard, magic charm,
rocked by storm, tempestwrecked, we've come as guests;

free will, hire cars, charter flights, fast ferries
have all conspired to speed us to this isle,

where once monks praised their God. We celebrate
an earthly bond, a pact, a confirming

of what is, in fact, a fact, a sharing
of vows and promises, a leap into

the known, the unknown, the unknowable.
All here in the unmoving scented heat,

witnessed by nesting gulls, lizards, poppies,
by cypresses, rosemary, yellow broom,

all here to applaud a union, a choice –
no man's an island – we were meant to find

a mate, cross the causeway at low tide. Now
there are no monks, just a man, a woman,

and we who watch, hope, toss our rose petals
in a monastery garden, saving

this day on camera, in memory.

A turquoise dress

Is very nice, Madame. You like,
yes? You look very nice...you like,
Madame, you like? Last night you dreamt

of a turquoise dress, buying it
with me, for me, all tissue wrapped,
placed in a glossy cardboard box.

Island fever's hunkering down
like a stowaway in steerage:
this might be paradise but still

we're bound by sky and sea. Ten days,
ill-at-ease with so much leisure
and you, who loathe shopping, propose

this trip, despite the heat; escape
by ferry to the mainland town
for retail therapy. Later,

parched, flushed, the gamut run from pastel
blue to teal, from silk to chambray
and back again, my body stripped,

found lacking, as I buy French navy,
unboxed, just a carrier bag
with twisted handles. We motor home

to our sanctuary, half-board, water-locked,
charge-it-on-the-room. *Is very nice,*
Madame. You like, Madame, you like?

No rain in the desert

Call it an epiphany, but not
in a good way - revelation of death
not of birth: that man with the Mr Blobby towel,
he made her realise it was over.
Raining when *you* went there too, August not
January...see mirage, ride camels, camp

by the oasis, watch sunrise over dunes,
a side dish of that Star Wars village. Like them,
you'd stayed in that desert hotel; expecting
sun; windowless, a sheet, one thin blanket,
as they'd planned for heat. You were ill-prepared,
underpacked for justabovefreezing,

Saharan storms. It's late in the bar outside. This
is what we all have in common, apart from just
being here – we were sold the dream,
Lawrence of Arabia, seventeen degrees,
or eighteen, no less, and no, it *never* rains
in January. Maybe light showers. We came,

were surprised, got drenched, and I picture you
changing out of wet trousers, swaying
in a coach aisle, while, further back, a large man,
fellow sopping traveller, does the same, clutching
his Mr Blobby towel, *her* finding it all so
distasteful, having that Damascus moment,

knowing it's over. Sometimes holidays help, quality
time, change of scenery, but sometimes they give
clarity, focus, that day - the Mr Blobby towel.

Elvis

Elvis, an encounter

Darkness over ripe Welsh meadows,
las vegas, fretted

by strings of fairy lights, solar, blue,
along May hedges, elder-greening, blossom-bursting,

by cigarette glow,

by crackling and hissing of logs from the firepit –
where folks huddle warmed by blankets, chat, whisky.

Well met by moonlight, proud incarnation,
thrusting the King's torch, rocking 'n rolling,

owning that suit, spritelike guest
at this night's nuptials, starblest,

incandescent, lighting up
the loin-lost gaze of his admirers,

who have seen a vision, divine
and otherworldly, (in fact from Malta),

shimmying gifts - lyric, liquidity
of hip, of lip, filling full his luminous leathers.

Now, far from home, awaiting his team,
he shivers in built-up shoes –

I AM NOT COLD; I HAVE PERFORMED.

Elvis takes his leave, cash, applause,
his black truck back,

not loving us tender yet still weaving
some chill, silvery spell,

as tail-lights reveal
sequins shed on bluebell, cow parsley and nettle
at the field gate,

our lane pitted with stardust.

Kyrenia

Arrival

It's been fifteen hours since the alarm, ten
since we handed over keys, lane eight,
got wedged between newer, larger, smarter cars;
and what a bargain - valet-parking - same price
as long stay. Check-in. Flight delay. Seven hours
from when it should have been.

Kill time. An ogling fest, a buying fest,
olfactory assault in harsh tax-free, picking
at breakfast, queueing, and then queueing
some more. Waiting. Killing time. Fifteen hours
since the alarm. Ninety minutes since the driver came,
his name the same as Welsh for fire. Leather seats,

the smell of alien cigarettes, smooth EU roads,
try to sleep, fail and then the border. He sorts it out,
disappears into the dark with passports, returns
with them and two scruffy slips, thin paper bearing
the all-important stamps. *Don't lose these.*
Ninety minutes of a small screen, dance music,

writhing bodies, Disneyesque cartoons, a blast
of entertainment thoughtfully provided. Fifteen hours
and here we are, flotsam on a badly grouted foyer floor,
blinking into sputtering yellow lights. They wax; they wane.
A slow check in, very slow, aching for room, two coffees,
bed and loo. The midnight shift insists we eat two plates

of something warmed and left to cool, drink
two tepid complimentary drinks. We do our best, smile
wanly at the other four force-fed late arrivals,
blindly follow this boy. A cramped lift, a clumsy fumble
with a key. Observe with no surprise street lights,
street noise, twin beds, thin curtains which don't quite meet,

that step sited to trip the unwary in the night.
This is not how it's meant to be. Sixteen hours.
Tomorrow we'll find the front desk, ask for Sarah,
who will change the room, make it right, but now
we're both too tired to care. There's just
the pressing need for sleep.

Leonardo di Caprio

We've already read about the oranges
on the plane, so, next morning we're unfazed
to find them green, all green.

The only orange orange here is the juice
which isn't. Instead, it's sweetened, cloying,
the colour added to beguile us, British guests.

We're a motley bunch – Germans, Italians,
half a dozen Brits, outnumbered by the Eastern Meds,
all tans, gold, sparkle and glamour.

So many heels breaking their fast. So little
of the slapslack casual we expect. We are pale,
grey, creased and underdressed.

Look, there's a Russian gangster and his whipslick moll.
Look, there's a pair of wealthy silver surfers
in the sun. She's smoking; he takes his coffee black.

They've been here a while; they both sport shades
at breakfast. Table linen, all crisp, bleached white,
is cluttered by the toys of Western leisure,

Western commerce, smartphones, laptops, kindles
with supporting casts - those chargers, headphones, cables,
while, on his own, *don't look,* it's Leonardo.

Is it uncool to stare, there, past the basking mother cat,
her kitten? You don't think he smokes but here he is.
It must be right. An open pack of twenty, red,

a large coffee and a paperback. No gadgets here.
Nothing flash. Just the shape of his face,
that deep groove between his brows, And yes,

he's built. Solid. Somehow you always thought
him slighter. Wait – that sauntering waiter, the one
who doesn't look quite right, like this is his choice,

the being here. Wait! He blocks your view,
and then you hear the voice, see the thinning crown.
This man is older, doppelganger,

an unknown prince. Am I the only mortal
who delights in trickery, in might-have-beens,
like this?

Visitation

Last night tall gods flew amongst us.
We were in their presence, captive, blessed.
There were six of them. One boy god
in human disguise, with hoodie, backwards cap,
a little bling, swaggered the length of our dull silver bird,
front to back, towered above the purple headrests, heads,
hair. God of sport mayhap? A prince of basketball?

Zeus, meanwhile, was in extra legroom, standing mostly,
watching, dark stubble long enough to be soft,
shoulder-length locks curling at the nape
of that so regal neck; smouldering, through half-closed
sleepy eyes. Three wives, a younger fourth,
her status unknown, went about their goddess business,
with loud chattering, frequent tossing of lustrous manes,

dwarfing the lolling, the napping, fish-flapping mouths,
wailing red babies and masses of the careless crumpled,
with heads wired to a beat, to a baseline.
We earthlings get bounced at last
to a final, unseemly standstill; brush off crumbs, smooth clothes
with sleep-skewed hair, gather all belongings, devices.

Switch on. Switch on. Ragtaggle shuffle
to passport control, baggage collection,
earthly officialdom, the world outside, night.

And what of our deities,
all unruffled glamour? Into thin air, of course.
We'd expected nothing less.

Crooner

He loves us tender, shares that last waltz,
is lonesome tonight, perhaps every night,
celebrates blue skies, blue birds, blueness
over cliff and rainbow. He thinks to himself
what a wunnerful world it is.

He croons in transatlantic, panEuropean
with few consonants, none of those final ones,
plays sax between his vocals, abetted,
haphazardly, by a dour Turk on keyboards.
A set for hybrid diners,

replete with sun, wine and food. There is just enough
for us to recognise, fill in the gaps,
hum along, clap. As *you* observe, we are mostly
in our mid and later years, the Brits and Germans
older than the rest.

There's a team of uniformed locals, *seen it,*
heard it all before, all season, who smile little,
except for those flirting with the loudest,
oldest, mostly solo matrons. Selling their souls
for hopes of final parting tips.

The more reserved, like us, observe this pantomime,
down another beer, another Disaronno,
retire to book and sunburn cream and bed,
the second promise of an upgrade,
that smooth and soothing, seam-free superking.

The second day

Holidays - it's been a while. This is how
it's done. Your stomach gurgles and protests,
sweet orange, hard plums, a surfeit of grapes,
spiced olives, saltless cheese and light soft rolls
with pumpkin seeds. Too much at breakfast.

Too easy to stay connected to life back home.
You're fretting about things left – not packed,
not enough, misplaced and just forgotten.
You've gotten out of the habit of doing this –
there's still a list of absentees, family, pets,

guests, plenty for you to worry about if this
is what you have in mind as relaxation.
And what about to-do instructions: were there enough?
Were they clear? Will they be heeded, followed,
ticked? Too early to let go yet.

And your daughter, barely six days wed;
is all in Sicily well? You could go
for a walk, explore, plop into the pool. Your bags
remain unpacked, rumpling further with each second,
but you've been promised a new room at two. Silly

to get too settled. Your man is splayed, sprawled,
barely conscious – that happy knack – but will snap
into busy tourist action at ten past two, scoff
at your need to unpack, refold, nest. The safe,
little sachets of Nescafe, grenades of longlife milk.

He'll be rushing you but you'll still want the call,
checking in so you can get a pass to check out. For now,
you baste, your pale pelt recalls what sun feels like

at noon. Listen to the poolside couple, oiling each other,
idling with a hotel cat. How fine the fur, the hair

that clings to flesh, clothes, towels, bed linen.
Your mind's still coiled but indolence begins
to glide over warmed skin. Nine more days.
You'll do it; you'll get there. Yes.

Settling in

We're moving our plastic chairs to catch
the last of the sun, on our second book,
you, a novel, me, history, but not too heavy.

Green oranges are now the norm, our indolence
has lost the power to shock. Boredom's not yet raised
her head to ruffle doing nothing. No news from home.

Vague disquiet; hard to trust that all is well
without being told. As usual, I've packed no teabags,
too few emollients to soothe parched flesh.

Try not to dwell on the jacuzzi. What we hoped
was just a missing fuse, is not. It doesn't WARK,
we're told with shrugs. We need to accept

just that - it's obviously policy, a no-bubble,
hotelwide decree. There is a time to stress.
This isn't it. We have here all we need.

Kitten

The feline on your lap is scrawny, maybe six
or seven months. If that. He's on his own. You've nothing
for him really. He's turned up late for leftovers.

Your server's fussing at another table while
chatting to two men, dressed in black, playing backgammon.
From time to time, she shoots a glance across,

in case you need something else. You find the kitten
just a few crumbs, no more, and he eats
with delicacy, deliberation. Nothing is wasted.

Already, there's a swelling on one side
of his mouth. It's met with tooth or claw. There's a scab
at the base of his tail, another halfway down his back.

A larger, sleeker cat watches from a distance,
relaxed, but primed for action. You think of soft-bellied pets
back home. This scrap of life, he's not had time, yet,

to grow into those huge, pale eyes,
that long, ratty tail. It may not happen. This lap,
this hand stroking the kitten's chest, his head, his ears,
this is a brief reprieve from the daily business
of survival. You've nothing for him really.

Castle

Guilt slinks in this morning. We must do something,
see something, go somewhere. So we relent,
take the half hour supposed ten-minute walk
to town, work hard at not stumbling
on broken kerbstones. This surface less surprising,
more familiar now.

And here's the castle, here for a thousand years,
maybe more, bulwark against sea and sky, fortress
to repel invading hordes. Crumbling yellow stone,
naked of barriers, warnings, no information
in any language. Health and safety's
not yet landed. We wander, tagging on

to straggles of tourists, locals, Germans,
Swedes, in hopes of scraps of knowledge.
We learn little except the admiral's tomb,
shipwreck remains from three millennia back.
Samos, Kos, Rhodes, then almost here.

Sharing only a few of its secrets – grape pips,
almonds, fig seeds, a few amphorae pieced together.
Stories, lives, just fragments left. That voyage
ending so abruptly.

Mother tongue

You haven't even got your brain around
the alphabet yet: you hear the constant shushing
and chooking, complicated consonants starting,
interrupting, finishing what must be words.
A whisper, a caress, an exclamation.

In writing, accented letters confuse you too,
but there's something soothing in these...
unknown sounds, not overtly emotional,
conveying information, instruction, a point
of view, not making much of it. No fuss.

The long sigh of history.

Permanent resident

At breakfast today you're told about the man,
white hair, walks with a stick,
(not much help in pinpointing here),
about ninety, who lives as a permanent resident
in this hotel.

You've heard about this back home,
the eccentric, the exceptionally rich,
ancient loners who choose to wither
with half-board, room service, pared-down possessions,
nothing left to part with.

But here *he* has sun. Perhaps it works
for as long as you can dress yourself,
deal with the basics of toilet, bathing, getting
in and out of bed unaided.

You're thinking in particular
of the vast bath in your room,
once a jacuzzi, sadly no longer.
To climb in, for one as vertically challenged
as you, is exactly that, a challenge.

At ninety, you doubt you'd manage.

Another castle

Across the wide brown plain, up, winding,
but a new smooth road, up and up again,
through cypresses, fringed with yellow broom, we climb.

Another castle, promise of a pitstop, a coffee,
maybe lunch. Maybe not. Just five lire, a portacabin loo,
a sign about protected flora, fauna.

Once this end of the island was rich in oak. You see
pictures of large long acorns, spread by jays.
Now there are few birds, but cats undulate

between parked cars. So many cats. On your ascent
you've been talking about the Lionheart, others
who led, invaded, held, fell, how much

determination you would have needed to fight here,
when you could be seen coming down mountains,
across the plain, and to the sea, the climb

there would have been just to get here, no matter
the ascent to the base of castle walls. Forget the scaling,
the breaching. It's amazing that you'd bother,
that any cause would have meant enough.

Stake *your* claim, now the German couple's left,
to the picnic bench below that cypress shade, two tabbies
prone on gravel to your right. They show no interest.
You have no feast to share. And there's a blue hatchback.

From an open window, strains of some soft Turkish song,
not disturbing any peace. A mew, a sigh of breeze,
a louder murmur from the rocks below. A lone bird call.

No voice of man. No cicadas. And the rocks before you,
limestone again, they form a natural castle, a fort perhaps
as impressive as the one *you've* refused to climb.

The blue car's owner is the man who mans the plastic booth,
pre-fab. He's had his power nap. He leaves the cats,
semi-recumbent, watchful. The wind picks up,

fanned and bellowed between the cypresses,
whirling about the fortress stones. Your man returns, replete,
content, five lire worth of ruins, well spent.

Woman in olive tree

The last ladder you saw being used
in earnest
was at that basilica -
a wooden ladder, tall and flexing,

with a woman at its narrow top,
a woman clad in long shirt, long skirt,
cardigan, her head scarved,
harvesting olives,
talking non-stop to her man below,
careless of peril,

while the child and the scabbed cat played
amongst the ruins.

Swallows

It could be a private party; four women,
a courtyard roofed with vines and fenced
with terracotta pots, festooned with lanterns,
some souk-ish style. We're beckoned in,

for this is, after all, a watering hole, where notes
will change hands, where the woman who
addresses us, is in the business of refreshment,
serving thirsty travellers. And we explain,

as though it's required, that we are strangers
to these parts. One of them lives here,
the one whose garden we're in, plying
her trade as a foreigner. Her parents bought in '48.

She came back in the 80s, after the troubles,
tried to settle, make a go of it. The others state
they're swallows.
We come and we go, whenever we can,
but never in the summer. Three weeks at least
in springtime. Again, this time of year.

We've heard this several times, these last few days,
people who keep coming back, as if rooted
to this place. If it wasn't incorrect, completely,
you might call them 'game old birds.'

But it is, and so, of course, you don't. And something
strikes you about how brave it is, making a life
up here, as you drive back that night
to safety, lights, what you've come to know.

Normally

Normally, it doesn't rain here
till January. *But look,* she says,
showing you the black moist soil
around the roots of a tree.

I've not watered it. It's the rain;
it's come early, but then that's climate change.
Everything's different now.

And two of the women nod in agreement,
wrap themselves, one shawl, one pashmina,
(from Tina Pashmina in the market),
feeling Autumn's chill.

Unfinishing

So much of what you see is unoccupied,
maybe built on spec and only finished when
a buyer can be found. Maybe. Or a sign

of these economic times: builder's gone
to the wall: someone's broke. This is the norm,
not the exception. Everywhere it seems you drive,

eyeless shells line your route, structures put up,
rendered, then left incomplete. It unsettles you.

Geckos, praying mantis, snake

It was sitting on the arm
of her garden chair, as she read
her one-day-late paper. She indicates
which chair, so we can all picture
the scene.

Its triangular face had seemed
to follow her face, move when she moved,
tilt when she stood up.

Her friend had a drama in the shower,
a gecko in residence,
who needed moving first.
They like it inside. The women all agree
there's not *much* wrong with geckos.

And someone talks about
the remains of a snake, brought back
in triumph by a cat.
Not much left to identify it,
other than as snake.

Geckos and praying mantis
are forgotten, as we shudder,
ophidiophobic, in unison.

The wall

You forget the name, but someone, a man,
a local builder, built her a walled defence,
and it was because of the rain,
the winter deluge, an attempt to divert
the torrents from her house and land.

A thick, strong wall, now all in the garden,
too heavy to shift. A night time drunk,
who took the bend too sharply, crashed
into stone. *At least it was there,* she says,
or it would have been her bedroom.

Look, you can see the tyre marks on the wall!
She'll dine on her celebrity for months, almost
making up for the waste – time, money and effort -
the certain chaos which will come again with rain
next winter. She shivers. A lucky escape.

Look, you can see the tyre marks!

Dare

We're here for a rest, end-of-the season.
They're here rediscovering old haunts, warm,
together. A crisp, silvery couple
we can't fail to notice. Tables move closer.

In the thickening dark, he speaks, we listen,
she smiles. We all drink a bit too much.
He was stationed here.

Back then he'd buzz the end of this island;
they all did, testing their skills, boys, young men
at most, with their metal toys.

Only a handful of monks left, a farmer
or two, scraping subsistence from this hostile soil.
Donkeys, of course, who ***would*** *voice their ire.*

They'd fire rockets as well, into the sand,
flexing muscle and nerve, while this man's wife
and children picnicked in the dunes.

Wave to Daddy and his friends. And they'd watch
a small boy dash from nowhere to grab
his spoils, the brass shells, take them home

to his village to be pooled, then sold. Timing
was everything; run, drop, collect, retreat
before the jets returned. There must have been

accidents. She doesn't remember, just her girls
in flowered dresses, the wicker hamper,
happy times.

Pool shoot

Hard to hear it all, your ears half under water.
Four of them, ruddy, bronzed, weather-beaten,
again discussing packing, where to put
the dirty stuff – *just chuck it in* – but suddenly,
you're treading water, and there on the old well

there are cameras and folk who aren't tourists.
At first you see her back view only, extended arm
behind her head, a small tattoo at nape of neck,
bright scarlet and orange hair piled high. Arms
braceleted generously, long legs striking poses,

fragile below the micro skirt, above – *how can she*
walk in them? - those high stacked sandals. He's weary,
worn, overdressed, shirt, tie, high-waisted tailored trousers,
perhaps, thirty, forty years her senior. He hangs
two heavy cameras across his chest, carries

a third. Much clicking. Another minute and she's gone,
inside, and back again, over her arm a bathing suit
in unknown animal print, a short, sequinned dress.
They pause to pet one of many cats weaving
between sunloungers, speculate again about...

that Cheryl Cole – what does she do?
What's she famous for? You labour back,
not an expert on celebrity, just always eavesdropping,
out of practice at swimming, other things too.

Low season

The dining room echoes, so few of you here now.
It's barely half past ten. There's just one family
next door in the TV and games room,
a single child here, doted on
by parents, grandmother
and an over-attentive waiter who dances with her.

It's music night again, with the repertoire stretched
rambling and blending roses, my way,
you were always on my mind,
karaoke lyrics, a cod American drawl...

Just after the fly-swatting, *that fearsome woman*
bent on extermination, who made cutlery shudder,
shake, rattle and roll on several tables,
just before the tour party returned with brochures,
day-sacks, canvas bags, cameras,
and angry reddened skin,

and just after the tabby-and-white kitten, lonesome
tonight and always, tolerated in the gardens,
not allowed indoors for reasons, perhaps, such as this,
jumped into a large blue glazed pot, prepared his spot,
earth flying, defecated neatly then dug, scrabbled, buried
the evidence except, of course, its pungent aroma,

leapt down and away between tables
to gales of Western laughter,
our musicians switched to French, ignoring
our merriment, mostly playing sad songs
we couldn't quite place.

But these two, our minstrels, seemed now more at ease
than in their set of transatlantic standards.
You left them crossing continents,
felt watched by countless feline eyes,
in night time camouflage,

as you crossed the courtyard to your cool, dark room.

A little scrap

Hard to recall what it was even about,
our brief bicker in this Eden. It took
another kitten to melt the atmosphere,
trigger a thaw.

He jumped onto the flat roof, from there
to metal balcony railings,
and through the open door,
onto your bed, all effortlessly,

seeking pastures new, food, adventure,
love. Without fear. The two of you play with him,
tease him with feet and hands
through the thin cotton sheet,

take photographs, stroke him, laugh.
Whatever it was, long gone.

Derek

You've had two uncles, one by marriage, with this name
so '***Derek'*** snarled from the pool below, it breaks the spell
of sun and book and laziness. It's a week on;
you're uncoiling. This break is doing what it's meant to do.

They're younger than you thought they'd be, awkward
on loungers, with a day to kill before their airport transfer,
no appetite left for killing, except each other. She jabs the air.
What're you doing with these, Derek?

She points at a pair of well-worn trainers, blue, male,
with some distaste. *I'm packing them; they're comfortable.*
His voice is quiet but you know he'll brook no change of plan,
no diversion. This tourist's not for turning.

No way, she hisses.
Too old, she hisses.
They smell, she hisses.
No room, she hisses.

At this he waves a forefinger towards
a small, black canvas bag.
Carry on, he says. *She* gathers herself, summons logic,
volume, venom.

*But you can't wear sandals on the plane. We're landing
at two. It'll be dark and cold and wet. Derek, you can't.*

His response is mild but I feel his steel.
You don't know that.

You mark my words, Derek. But no words come.

Derek has grown. *They're coming with me, and that's final.*
My feet won't mind.
You return to your book: something
has been settled.

Yellow wellies

There's a name for this kind of saw,
long and curved, designed to hook
round each branch of the palms.
A guy in jeans, striped shirt, a cap
and yellow wellies is up a metal ladder,
sawing branches off the trees.

Perhaps they cast too much poolside shade?
Perhaps they cut the space too much
for bronzing, dozing guests?

Maybe they just grow so fast it must be done
each year. It seems a shame, too harsh,
too radical.

Yellow wellies' two accomplices
marshal the limbs into big bunches,
tie lengths of rope around the opposite ends
to those no-longer-waving fronds,
drag them, four or five at once
around the edge of the pool
and away.

Yellow wellies now perches on the roof
over the ping-pong table,
surveys his ferny hoard, the fruits
of his destruction.

They have moved from palms
to a general pruning. Too soon, this easy abundance
will be manicured, pedicured,
trimmed and tamed.
You regret the necessity.

Dip

Strange that at this time of year
it's dark at half past five. Six days ago
clocks went back. You chase the last rays
to a corner of the pool, by the bins, close
to the man who mows constantly,

taking half a day to do very little.
Not big on subtlety, two other guys
are pulling off cushions, dragging sun-loungers
to their night-time cribs,
pointedly leaving just your two and two
at the other end, filled by
an older pair, who are either oblivious, don't care
or both.

They're offering support from the side-lines
to their friend, who arrives each day
for a stately late afternoon swim, after all jumpers,
splashers and shriekers have gone.

No sun on the water, and the chill stuns
as you slip in. But with that miracle
of submersion it becomes first bearable, then
unremarkable.

You're no longer listening to the hum
of homeward traffic, to Aphrodite's fountain,
to muffled voices round the courtyard bar.

You're hanging up a wet costume in the still air,
sharing a small beer, a pine-scented glass of wine,
aware of the absence of cats, so rare now,
the muezzin's call, the fact that all things pass.

Lawrence Durrell's bar

It's dark, and the narrow streets have emptied
without us noticing. No taxis by the abbey.
The two numbers on the board are unobtainable,
so we hail the only taxi to go by. He's booked,
but he stops, makes a call, tells us to look
for a silver car, in fifteen, twenty minutes.

This is the tree of idleness, opposite the abbey
and this is where we choose to wait.
A glass of red, a glass of white, liberally filled
by the Thai girl, the one who isn't...
sweeping woodshavings.

We've arrived as another tree, not
the tree of idleness on the corner,
another tree is chainsawed from the bar.
It has not been idle. It's grown from a lean,
an inclination across the threshold,

up to the first floor, through the white ceiling,
to the restaurant upstairs. How many people
does it take to sever these rogue branches?
One to wield the chainsaw, three
to offer helpful advice, one, possibly the manager,

to balance on a table, wiggling what's left
down through the hole in the ceiling, and two
black suited girls, one to sweep
and one to serve. Rounds of wood are lifted out,
carried away by another helper. This tree

grew too well, too thick, too tall,
in the wrong place, in a bar and restaurant

which claims its link, a faded poster
about Lawrence Durrell, even though *this man*
has lost his final 'l'.

He was here from '53 to '56. We wonder when
this tree was planted, how long it's taken,
what stories it's witnessed. The manager
is happy now. A silver car draws near
and there's been something novel

about waiting in the dark, drinking wine,
to the music of a chainsaw.

And afterwards...

After the challenges of Covid we have more-or-less returned to the numbers and sizes of weddings we were hosting pre-pandemic. There have been changes and there are always challenges. But the business continues, now, increasingly, under the watchful eye of my daughter and her chef husband.

We moved to a cottage at the foot of our land – Troed-y-Rhiw – just over eighteen months ago. And when I unpacked one box I found the Kyrenia notebook and starting using it as the inspiration for a group of linked poems. I've topped and tailed them with a few others, travel and wedding themed. And, of course, Elvis!

We've not yet been back to Kyrenia but it felt like respite and renewal for us as a couple. A cwtch indeed.